Letters to the Leader

*poems written in response to the 55 Executive Orders
from Donald J. Trump's first year as President
of the United States of America*

Letters to the Leader

*poems written in response to the 55 Executive Orders
from Donald J. Trump's first year as President
of the United States of America*

*by
HanaLena Fennel*

- 2019 -

Letters to the Leader
© Copyright 2019 HanaLena Fennel
All rights reserved. No part of this book may be used or reproduced in any manner whatsoever without written permission from either the author or the publisher, except in the case of credited epigraphs or brief quotations embedded in articles or reviews.

Editor-in-chief
Eric Morago

Associate Editors
José Enrique Medina, Michael Miller, Ellen Webre

Marketing Specialist
Ellen Webre

Proofreader
Jim Hoggatt

Front cover art
Unvesseling in paper and watercolor by HanaLena Fennel

Author photo
Marcus Anthony Kennedy

Book design
Michael Wada

Moon Tide logo design
Abraham Gomez

Letters to the Leader
is published by Moon Tide Press

Moon Tide Press #166
6745 Washington Ave., Whittier, CA 90601
www.moontidepress.com

FIRST EDITION

Printed in the United States of America

ISBN # 978-0-9974837-9-6

*to my ducklings
and darlings*

Contents

Foreword by Ben Trigg	13
Second Body	15
Click in paper and ink	16
Sitelines	17
To the Profane	18
The Meal is a Lie	19
Man as Tree	20
Ethics	21
Low in the Water in Ink	23
Dedication	24
At Weehawken	25
Indelicate	26
Counterintuitive Math	27
Upbringing	28
Tall Tales	29
B-52	30
Time Management for Hydrophobic Crabs	31
Sustenance	32
Shekhinah	33
Wake in Ink	34
Because Crows Come in Murders	35
This.	36
Ask in Ink	37
Three Miracles to Sainthood	38
Policy	40
Cuerpo de Amor	41
Four Poems for a Husband	42
The Shadow of Sufferance Flutters Divination /	43
Love, Money, and Even Death	44
Untitled in Ink	45
In Her Piety	46
Cicadas	47
Body	49
Arrowhead in Ink	50
Untitled	51
How Today Finds Me	52
Restless in Ink	54

Language	55
Berth	56
Story Keeper	58
Figurehead in Ink	59
So, You're Living in a Weekly Rental	60
The President Explains Promise-Keeping to a Dreamer	61
Render	62
This Love	63
Norman Rockwell's *The Happy Plumber*	64
Being Pregnant at Papa's Funeral	65
Reach in Ink	66
Stardust	67
Sepia	68
Hello in Ink	69
Long Term House Issues	70
Seven Lies	71
Prompt	72
Parts	73
How Not to Silence a Mother	75
Sailor	77
Pre-Script	78
Blue	79
Diagnosis: Unspecified Effects of Drowning and Nonfatal Submersion, Initial Encounter	80
Sea Voyage	81
Placeholder	82
Letter to B~	84
Untitled in Paper and ink	85
Snake Eaters	86
Michael Powell's Peeping Tom	87
Plate of Bones in paper, vellum, and oil paint	88
Skeleton Key	89
Acknowledgements	90
About the Author	91

Foreword

You are holding a year's worth of trauma in your hands. A year's worth of fear and horror at the cruelty and incompetence of a man in power. A decision to make art as self-defense. A decision to make art as healing. Art as comfort and balm for both the author and the reader. HanaLena Fennel took her natural bent as a policy wonk and chose to synthesize legalese into poetry. She doesn't tell us what Trump's executive orders say, she shows us how a fully functioning heart feels after reading them.

Now you know what you're about to read. You didn't really need me to tell you about it. It's like three pages away. I'm really here to tell you about HanaLena Fennel. About the kind of person who would spend a year tying their creative-self to Donald Trump so the rest of us don't have to. HanaLena is loud and bold, kind and gentle. I hesitated to tell you she's loud because that's the kind of adjective that gets used as an insult, but here's the secret of her volume: it's an invitation to become part of the conversation. It says, "I'm not keeping anything from you. You are welcome here. You belong." I am one of the hosts of Two Idiots Peddling Poetry. I sit at the front because I have to, but new people terrify me. HanaLena is not one of the hosts. She sits at the front because she chooses to. She engages new people in way I never could. She is the welcoming committee. She sees you nervously approach the sign-up sheet for the first time? You're family now, and she's going to make sure you know it.

Opening this book makes you family of a sort. It is an invitation to see the human scale of the Trump administration; to look past the headlines and the legal maneuvers so we can feel the truth of today's America. It is a reminder that we are all in this together. You've probably heard "the personal is political," but with this collection, HanaLena makes the political personal. She takes the (sometimes inscrutable) policy of the President and applies it to her life and the lives of those she loves. She tells you her story so that you may have a guide through your story. The political is personal for you, too.

I am so excited for this book. And so proud to see it finally here. As in most things HanaLena does, it is an invitation to belonging, that you aren't alone in your fear, that there is comfort to be had, and that all of us have the power to stand up for what is right.

— Ben Trigg, co-host of Two Idiots Peddling Poetry

January 20, 2017
Executive Order 13765
Minimizing the Economic Burden of the Patient Protection and Affordable Care Act Pending Repeal

Second Body
a pre-existing condition

This hollow, in English, is to vessel;
        as in:
        I am a broken ghost ship trying to grow an ocean.

        Or:
        I entered this contract, the becoming a barge,
        belly low slung in the water,
        gravid with cargo, willingly,
        the journey less important than the destination
        of boy child, open eyes, on dry land.

This hollow is to vessel, as in:
no one could have known
hull and hollow are so close on the tongue,
and, being swallowed, rescue themselves as cruelties.

I used to carry here,
        to know myself as vessel
        and journey.

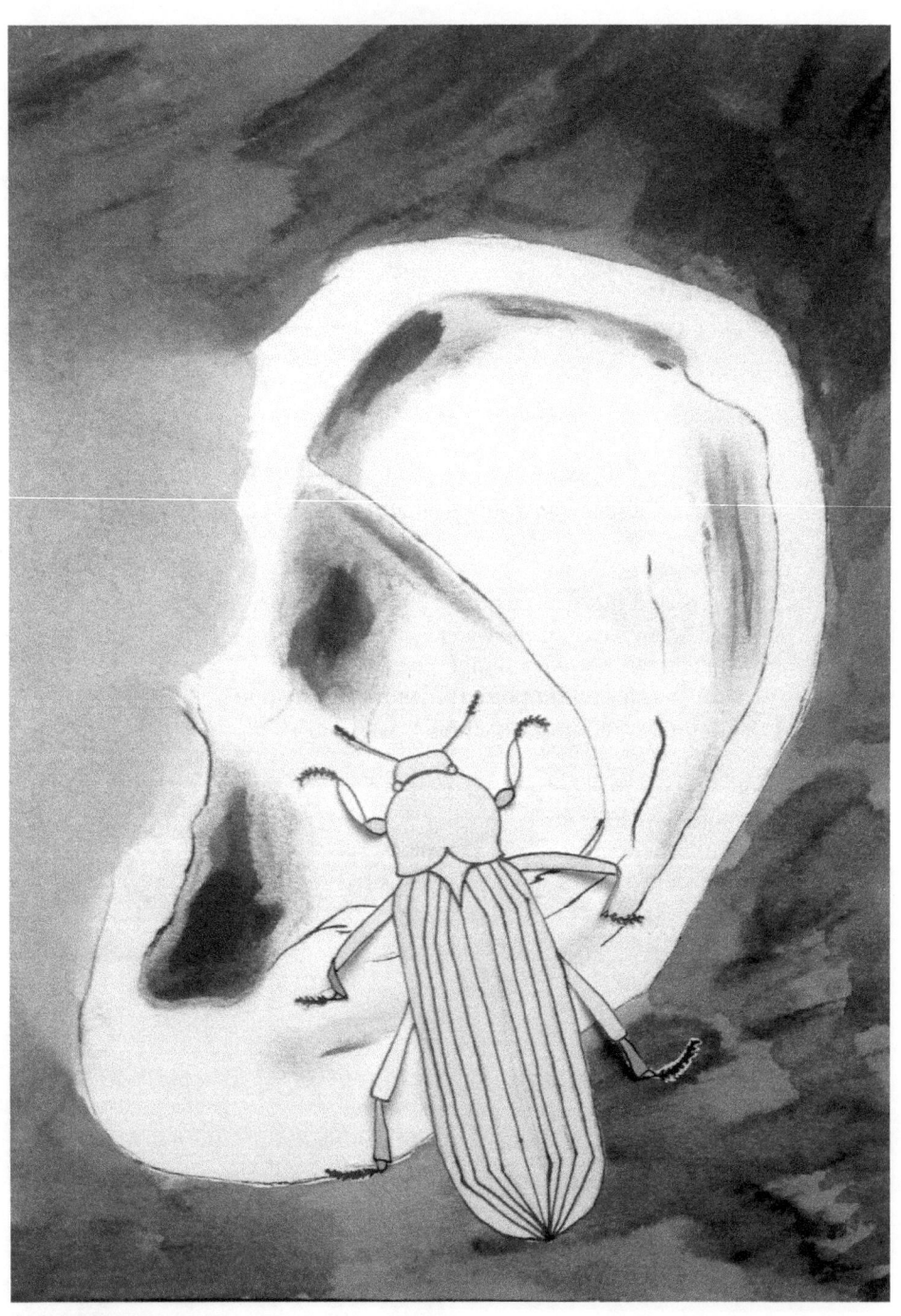

January 24, 2017
Executive Order 13766
Expediting Environmental Reviews and Approvals for High Priority Infrastructure Projects

Sitelines

They expedite
an empty-purse diesel-moth
to cartoon this flight up to you.

I am not sure you know yet
that these treasurers have teeth,
or gummy mouths,
lined with street lamps
and all lit up.

They huddle,
hundred-legged hunters.
These words, the haze and hum—
the huff-huff oratory of half-done.
Each tongue-flick,
a highway
to unsully four hundred and thirty-five facet-cut eyes.

This is the road we have actually funded.
Tar black to camera.
And back, camera
and back.

January 25, 2017
Executive Order 13767
Border Security and Immigration Enforcement Improvements

To the Profane

It likely began with a crook to hook the lamb—
    a serpentine teardrop river in the pasture.

In Hebrew, she is curved belly ל
    Arabic, a fishhook ل

It is a letter of *for*,
    for my father,
    for love.

Limāḏā, for what?

But also of *doing*, *to* speak, *to* grow.
    As *lomed*, to learn is to do,
    to do is to learn.

Elohim, for my father, for love, for what?
    To speak, to grow, to learn, to do.

January 25, 2017
Executive Order 13768
Enhancing Public Safety in the Interior of the United States

The Meal is a Lie

The meal is a lie. Fingernail crescents. Angel hairs. Sustenance.

Sustenance will never be these things we discard.

Discard the coil of a hello-tongue or last kiss.

Kiss the breath through sugared hands of child, of silence, of gimme.

Gimme surrender. Body prostrate before windmill.

This is not grain or flour. The lance is spent, piked in the wildflowers.

We have tilted, and the earth refused to budge.

January 27, 2017
Executive Order 13769
Protecting the Nation from Foreign Terrorist Entry into the United States

Man as Tree

While the explorers traveled, their homelands were often ablaze with the fires of persecution and war.

— Daniel L. Pals, *Seven Theories of Religion*

Should I feel guilty
that all my bridges
burned themselves
behind me?

Were you to rise late
and trek, slog through
the swamps of my past,
seeking out chunks of rotting wood,
you would find
all the ready signs of arson
are one-sided.

If metaphor can be memory,
lurk as detritus impersonating predator
and drift alongside body-love's faces
draped in Ophelia death gauze,
we could find your charred limbs,
skin still fire hot, fingers reaching for contact,
ready to roll and pull us under.

This wetland, body-love,
this dank and devouring mud, placid
lake gone fetid—it sucks the embers down.
Binds your wooden boy hands in moss
and calls us prayer.

January 28, 2017
Executive Order 13770
Ethics Commitments by Executive Branch Employees

Ethics

[Ethics]
    As a condition,
a position invested with public trust
I commit myself.

[Serve]
    What is your fear?
    What is your chasm-mouth slit-tongue voiceless howl?
    What does it have to do with a calling?
    How does it bring you to bent knee strange communion here?
    When do you verb yourself in the shadow of marble cast titans?

[Departure]
    I am covered by my former agency.
    I will abide.

[Foregoing]
    Accept the provisions
    as binding on me
    as definitions with respect to those whom such designations mean
agency.

[Foreign Client]
    You should've seen the other guy.

[Former Client]
    See above.

[Former Employer]
See triple modular redundancy, complex magical triangle, American death triangle,
sheer ice walls; holding on.

[Gift]
Un-tongued, de-goded, un-awarded, hungry in their absence, legacy-less, relapsed
remittance, relief.

[Pledge]
"I, _____, do solemnly swear (or affirm) that I will support and defend the Constitution
of the United States against all enemies, foreign and domestic; that I will bear true faith
and allegiance to the same; and that I will obey the orders of the President of the United States and the orders of the officers appointed over me, according to regulations and the Uniform Code of Military Justice. So help me God."

[Waiver]
The President or his designee may grant to any person a waiver of any restrictions
contained in the pledge signed by such person.

This order supersedes.

January 30, 2017
Executive Order 13771
Reducing Regulation and Controlling Regulatory Costs

Dedication

And finally,
the formidable debt of absence in the face of wondrous spirit,
a dedication to his favorite smoke-skinned blonde.

Stuff all the flames into the leftover ache,
the howling sorrow of your mouth.
Let a daughter's love ash—
each conversation a forest fire on her ice-skin tundra.

No honors for lank curled second place,
for Delphinite soot divinations,
for lips ever-chapped from the initial char of mother's kiss.

There is room for one enkindled woman's outline frame,
curved as fetal scorch.

February 3, 2017
Executive Order 13772
Core Principles for Regulating the United States Financial System

At Weehawken

Our arguments were never about ourselves.
My love the bullets.
Our liberty a countdown.

I cannot parse the sentence in a way that doesn't make it a love story to death.
My love, the bullets.
I was a rush and you were a wait,
but also, I was a hurricane and you were a weight.

What are you waiting for?

My Love,
               The Bullets.

February 9, 2017
Executive Order 13773
Enforcing Federal Law with Respect to Transnational Criminal Organizations and Preventing
International Trafficking

Indelicate

My communion,
strange and calm,
is the letting go of
this bit-tongue devotion.
Guilt,
as a full-mouthed wine of you.

Grief,
the snapping teeth of loss,
renders me down to the smallest parts.
Your black sky,
my voice is still lion
to fulfil a body's heritage.

I am swallowed prayer.
I did not agree to mourn you,
wear your forgetting as my skin.
An oracle unspeaking herself.

February 9, 2017
Executive Order 13774
Preventing Violence Against Federal, State, Tribal, and Local Law Enforcement Officers

Counterintuitive Math

In this proof,
expressed in the natural language,
there are three doors and stage lights.

The first door is painted a shade of blue that only exists
in surplus, or her eyes.
The second, the tear-salt caramel warm of hands.
You can't see the last door at all.

None of these lintels promise prizes on the other side.

Which one is the feel of wood scraping your lips, splintering
memory into flesh?
Which the heavy steel security of wound up too tight, or gunmetal
put-your-hands-up wound?
Can the blue be the sky, or escape, or failing?
Each aperture demands you have the body; body your burdens are the proof.

The door you don't see is both door and not-door at the same time.

This is both choice and not-your-choice.

Closing a door is not the same as un-opening.

February 9, 2017
Executive Order 13775
Providing an Order of Succession Within the Department of Justice

Upbringing
a found poem of quotes from Donald and Ivanka Trump

If being complicit means… [1]
Locker room banter [2]
You have to treat 'em like shit [3]
And when you're a star [4]
Grab them by the pussy [5]
Perhaps I would be dating her [6]
Quality for me is key [7]

My father values talent [8]
Low I.Q. crazy [9]
A special place in hell for… [10]
You are a pussy [11]
Hard to be a ten [12]
Gosh, I sound like my father [13]
That's part of the fun [14]

---

[1] Trump, Ivanka. Television Interview with Gayle King. *CBS This Morning*. CBS. April 5, 2017
[2] Trump, Donald. *Campaign Statement*. Donald Trump Presidential Campaign. October 6, 2016
[3] Trump, Donald. Told to friend Philip Johnson according to *New York Magazine*. 1992
[4] Trump, Donald. Video Recording with Billy Bush. *Access Hollywood*. NBC. 2005
[5] Trump, Donald. Video Recording with Billy Bush. *Access Hollywood*. NBC. 2005
[6] Trump, Donald. Television Interview. *The View*. ABC. March 6, 2006
[7] Trump, Ivanka. Online Interview with Andrew Bevan. Teen Vogue. March 28, 2012
[8] Trump, Ivanka. Listed as Headliner. 2016 Republican Convention. July 21, 2016
[9] Trump, Donald. Tweet. Twitter. June 29, 2017
[10] Trump, Ivanka. Interview with unnamed reporter from Associated Press. *Ivanka Trump says child tax credit 'not a pet project' by Catherine Lucey*. Associated Press. November 15, 2017
[11] Trump, Donald. Video Recording with Billy Bush. *Access Hollywood*. NBC. 2005
[12] Trump, Donald. Radio Interview with Howard Stern. *The Howard Stern Show*. WXRK. September 2005
[13] Trump, Ivanka. *The Trump Card: Playing to Win in Work and Life*. Touchstone. April 20, 2010
[14] Trump, Ivanka. Interview with Rachel Gillett. *Ivanka Trump describes her life as the daughter of a potential US president, running the Trump empire, and building her own brand*. Yahoo Finance. March 17, 2016

February 9, 2017
Executive Order 13776
Task Force on Crime Reduction and Public Safety

Tall Tales

When I was a child
America was full of giants.
Once a huge man with an axe
left footprints as large lakes in his wake,
ate through logging towns,
felled entire forests with a single swipe.
Worked better alone,
but always had his Babe.

The cowboy was never filmed with cows in the same shot.
That was left for off-screen vaqueros.
American Cowboys got stars and big guns.
Never missed.
Never left the shoot out to find those clapboard houses
offer no protection for the family cowering inside.
The child in the gingham dress is still a corpse
no matter which gang shot her.

The Hammer-man we loved for his size.
He was "too dumb to quit" even as it killed him.
Nobody worried about teaching his big black hands a skill.
We just cheered on from bandstands in the desert
as America's sacrificial gladiators fought the machines
that were meant to save him.

As a child, the only thing I learned of giants was
     they kill everything they love—
         die alone.
Sleep, giants.
Rest on the earth as mountains.
You were never really here.

And our gingham-dressed daughters have someplace to go.

February 24, 2017
Executive Order 13777
Enforcing the Regulatory Reform Agenda

B-52

My step-father still hears the wind
    when the music is off
      and the electricity is stolen back,
    felled like a tree one block over.

There was no hot, tropic zephyr
to blow that far up, to catch
his thick plastic marble cage hanging
expendable from the belly of a plane
built for shedding chunks of its cargo,
letting them plummet in air and gravity
'till fire could be the only resolution.

This high up,
he could not see the dense green,
thick tree heat, the patties
and quicksilver fish refusing to be caught up
and devoured between great elephantine teeth.

He has carried home
only the cirrocumulus breath,
the high whistling Santa Ana's
rattling against window panes
'till it is felt as a lover demanding entrance.

The thing about the wind, he starts,
is it's all the same,
traveling on gulfstream through troposphere
until it finds you again.

February 28, 2017
Executive Order 13778
Restoring the Rule of Law, Federalism and Economic Growth by Reviewing the "Waters of the United States" Rule

Time Management for Hydrophobic Crabs

The mussels have it easy.
They only have to hold on for dear life.
Let the water rush at them.
Grip fiercely against the tireless forces pushing them
toward a crushing death.
Be grateful for the food that comes in.

It's not the water they fear so much as the loss of control.
Here, everything is bigger than them.
Except for the truly tiny things.
The truly tiny things should be feared too.

It's not the water they fear so much as the crushing death.
Especially the crushing part.
The kind of pain that makes a gift of the nothing—
of the deep well of silence.

They plan for the tide.
Gathering round stones and broken homes.
Clutching them one at a time in clumsy pincers.
Stacking Hadrian's wall on the divide
between wet sand and safety.
The water comes; water finds a way.
The truly tiny things should be feared too.

February 28, 2017
Executive Order 13779
The White House Initiative to Promote Excellence and Innovation in Historically Black Colleges and Universities

Sustenance

I cannot eat your lips no matter how many times you press
them to mine
to offer kiss as communion.
This love is not a meal,
    a dining room table,
    a family painting.
We have caught up the bird in flight,
    great and angry red-tailed hunter,
        buried her in a rookery and called it home.
When the hood becomes new skin do you dream of a reflection
    covered in feathers and madness?
    The great screeching hunger of hunt?

I am famished, love.
My sorrow is a well down in my core.
Mouth to hollow gut.

I have devoured my cowl.
It was not enough.

March 6, 2017
Executive Order 13780
Order on Protecting the Nation from Foreign Terrorist Entry into the United States (revision of 13769)

Shekhinah

The stones are wailing,
or that sounds far past wailing
when grief scrapes the throat raw
and each breath is hoarse and hungry in the air—
when the stones of the wall slide against each other,
let go a moan of dust and gravel.

She is *zaftieg*, short and curvy,
all slopes and round hills,
with broad flat feet that plant themselves in the ground.
Her arms and legs are those of a mother,
used to having to do all the heavy lifting.
She does not need height.
The bridge to heaven is not long.

In the stories—all the husbands die first.
The children—left as souvenirs of love.
Each year's portrait is a postcard.

Wish you were here.

March 13, 2017
Executive Order 13781
Comprehensive Plan for Reorganizing the Executive Branch

Because Crows Come in Murders

L'amour est un oiseau rebelle...comme le sont vous, ma columbe

— Habanera, *Carmen*

Love is a rebellious bird...as are you, my dove.

This sound—corvid's ink wings, in their hungry push upward,
    could pull the gasp and ache
    from the space left behind.

You told me once you are the reincarnation of Amelia Earhart.
This is why you are afraid to fly.

This—the exhale of a forgiven breast,
    the release of hope as a curse on the world.

We were on an asphalt lake,
struggling against drowning in the air between us,
your eyes the blue of escape.

Sound—doves gone mourning in dusty earth shadow colors,
    plucking at each other's phantom wedding band necklaces,
    mistaking grief for death.

We began with the understanding that you cannot survive the biting cold.
You are already snowy colomdea wings and frost flower fingertips.
We are a series of little death collisions.
I set words to blaze.
Tongue forever poems on your skin in steam.
Scare a murder into flight.
And let lips shatter across thighs.

March 27, 2017
Executive Order 13782
Revocation of Federal Contracting Executive Orders

This.

This order
This order seeks
This order seeks to increase efficiency
This order seeks to increase efficiency and cost savings in the work performed by parties
who contract with the Federal Government by ensuring that they understand and comply

This order seeks to increase efficiency and cost savings in the work performed by parties
who contract with the Federal Government by ensuring that they understand and comply
with labor laws. Labor laws are designed to promote safe, healthy, fair, and effective workplaces.

This order seeks to increase efficiency and cost savings in the work performed by parties
who contract with the Federal Government by ensuring that they understand and comply

This order seeks to increase efficiency and cost savings in the work performed
This order seeks to increase efficiency
This order seeks
This order
This.

March 28, 2017
Executive Order 13783
Promoting Energy Independence and Economic Growth

Three Miracles to Sainthood

The miracle is your bite.
Each dirty mouthful
of sugary cereal, mayo sandwich,
her long finger sacrament,
paper wafers of flesh, and Moscato.
Your body has all the instinct for survival,
none for love.
Ever pushing at knives,
and needles,
and mothers that slept in fire.

Think then of story as equation,
a way of balancing,
trade crueler beginnings
for the better climax.
Suck in oxygen to exhale carbon ash.
Let the volcano eruption of birth
encase the dinette set,
all the chairs gone missing.
A family obvious in its absence.
Pause the hungry collision of teeth.

The miracle is your hatching.
Dusty velvet moth
painted poison butterfly colors
to keep the predators at bay.
This house is a hallway of doors,
each bed a cocoon—
grey but soft,
like the inside of wings

or sadness.
This evening, flight.
You only see your own underbelly—
are confused by words like beautiful.
Take in the possibility of landing.

The miracle is in my leaving.
In the full-mouthed love of you.
In the walking away.
In the coiled embrace of empty.
Of without.
Of smokeless nights.
Of my not saving.
Of silence.

Be not teeth or flight or fear of alone.

Rest.

March 29, 2017
Executive Order 13784
Establishing the President's Commission on Combating Drug Addiction and the Opioid Crisis

Policy

You are a glass jar.
The daughter of Sylvia Plath's oven portals.
Backstories are by definition
    the dead weight we carry behind.
All the mattresses full
    of Uncle Arties
        and twitching rabbit bodies.

They never write about how golden the desert is. How even the dying trees look like prayer hands, fingertips on the edge of G-d's immeasurable brow. I can love everyone here. Explode my luminous soul into forgiveness.

No one feels alone this close to death.

Life is hard for fate's light children.
The impossibly thin, purged of expectation.
The ones whom currents sweep away.

You are dark enough to hold down every memory.
Life is harder for the children too deep to drift ashore.

No one feels
        this close to death.

March 31, 2017
Executive Order 13785
Establishing Enhanced Collection and Enforcement of Antidumping and Countervailing Duties
and Violations of Trade and Customs Laws

Cuerpo de Amor

The body of flight, grounded.
Feathers in air are a freedom—
the soaring doubtless kiss of momentum.
In the hand, they are a corpse.

Blancas colinas,
there is no evidence of how I loved you
like planting seeds with greedy fingers,
burying desire in your bed.
The flowers between your thighs are not a painting for me.
I cannot sate need
by devouring stamen and pistil,
renaming them fruit and flesh.
I apologize then
to your hands,
still trying to take flight.
To the small coo of your voice,
the hollow between your breasts where,
    born shaft-less,
    I slowly pushed in my arrowheads,
    dug them in with my thumbs,
            and called them seeds.

March 31, 2017
Executive Order 13786
Regarding the Omnibus Report on Significant Trade Deficits

Four Poems for a Husband

Take one child, already born,
hands too small to cup your face.
Love her palms too young to form future telling lines.
This love a communion of fingertips.
Give normal
dad jokes, the warm hug of it's all alright.
The comfort of earth held steady.

Take bride, in blue and white polka dot dress,
belly already a swollen plum.
Give home.
A building and bed.
And crib to wait by.

Take smallest flesh of your flesh,
give skin-to-skin,
your high forehead and stubborn-love soul.

Take my cats, left side of the bed, school morning drop-offs, less
than half the closet, watch the kids—I need a night out, I tried
a new recipe, can you wash the dishes, get the trash, empty the dryer.
Give, give, give.

March 31, 2017
Executive Order 13787
Providing an Order of Succession Within the Department of Justice

The Shadow of Sufferance Flutters

Even if the steel could feel the wind,
she could not be a living thing, a tree in the tempest.
She could not release leaves like messages in a bottle,
each papery oval a plea for forgiveness.
Even if the sky were an ocean,
and your tears,
flying off cheeks
could find like kind,
water to water,
salt to the sea,
there are no islands on the horizon, rocky cove shorelines
to crash yourself into.

Even if the steel could feel the wind,
the cuts through air would make no lasting imprint.
Her stoic razor face is a temporary stopgap
against the miles-a-minute our globe turns through
space.

And if the wind could feel the steel,
it would still blow every ounce of itself to this moment.
There would be no holding back.
This conclusion was written in his opening gusts.

April 18, 2017
Executive Order 13788
Buy American and Hire American

Divination /
Love, Money, and Even Death

Love

When my step-father was a man, I wore lace threaded with soft pink velvet ribbons. We walked to the 7-11 for cowboy smokes so he could signal o-o-o rings to the night. He wore his hair down, all the way down, held my hand with fingers spattered the color of other people's houses and pulled his bottom lip in to scrape his teeth across the peak of his beard with a wet hiss like a warning snake, or deflating balloon.

Money

The green was better, even after he tore down my playhouse to use the concrete platform to grow. In the smoke, there was no falling ladder, no surgeons, no fucking Workman's Comp Appeals board. The lion's mouth drew the loops in tighter and smaller until his head fell to the table with a beer-can-mane rattle.

Even Death

My step-father's ghost piled our bones into big, black plastic trash bags. Mom's old high heeled feet went in. The ones she couldn't wear anymore. Not after he threw her into the hood of the Oldsmobile, splintering the nagging cello of her back. They were stuffed around the pooch of my child soft belly he had always warned would go to fat without discipline. To stop the clacking pair of female tongues and teeth castanet chomping, he stuffed in a faded blue bathroom, handed down from father figure to daughter shadow. He had neatly sharpied JEW PIG in the collar and tied a noose of the terry cloth belt. He dropped the garbage outside mom's work; assumed we brought our shovels.

April 21, 2017
Executive Order 13789
Identifying and Reducing Tax Regulatory Burdens

In Her Piety

Flight is a tangle of Fear and Air

Feast is Need gone ostentatious

Think of a breast as hands cupping pond water
Drink on tears and the first breaths from before man
or legs or lungs

Lips become hello
Without words we kiss ourselves into every encounter
Swallow the endings

When the menhaden are scarce
and have flashed their silvery tails to the inky green of deep water
she turns scavenger
hunting down frog prince and lady crab
and tears flesh from their mythical ever after

When fierceness fails
and no strength is enough for talons to grip a future
she turns Self into Self-Cannibal
Fishhooks her own salty breast with the curve of her beak
Drops heart's blood as rubies
into the cavernous mouths of her children

Feed
her wings whisper
Live

April 25, 2017
Executive Order 13790
Promoting Agriculture and Rural Prosperity in America

Cicadas

It's the clouds,
I think.
Each one laden with a thousand parchment wings to block out the sun.

It won't rain today.
The heat sucks the water from us,
lips and hands
cracked,
deadpan.

It's why she dreams of plagues,
of raspy-edged locust.
She sits, legs crossed and naked
in the desert,
her arms and lap overfull with wheat.
They descend.
One-by-one, primitively.
Alighting in her hair,
chirping arid melody, song raw and biblical,
narrow-clawed legs pirouetting on collarbones and fingertips.

She tells the story and
the dream starts to fill her.
She lifts in the bed, chest first,
letting the hotel sheet fall.
The curve of her breast,
honeyed globes,
makes me understand the eagerness of crude things to hurl their bodies at her.

We are at the part of the dream when the locusts become multitude.
They are heavier in her arms than the wheat was.
She cradles the angry weight of them like an infant,
and like a suckling they bite at her breasts.
Each nip an act of communion.
She is still as she bleeds for them.
I cannot help but think of the hunger of my own hands,
how they grip at her,
willing to devour her to sate my own need.

She does not hate the cicadas,
accepts that each rattling carcass of vellum acts according to its own nature.
She just wishes—
she says more to the air between us
than to me—
they could find another body to use.

April 26, 2017
Executive Order 13791
Enforcing Statutory Prohibitions on Federal Control of Education

Body

1
In time, you will learn
children are supposed to show as Kansas wheat fields.
Bob golden-headed in ready agreement.

I will raise you dark horse running.
Exhale words in cursive into your hips,
    bury in you movement like water.

2
We explored the curves of our spines through panic,
after a woman, rubbed thin and beige,
told us we might have been curving back into ourselves.
We pressed wildflowers, all bound together with broken questions,
into her fists, pulled down at the hem of her smile.
She was too in flight to notice, so we knew to trust her.
The only strangers to fear are the ones with time.

3
You grind your teeth in your sleep,
sanding my dreams into fine day dust.
And by princess night light,
    paint his handprints on your cave walls.

4
We all start with black and white.
Now you ask for yellow hair,
    so you can sleep till your eyes match my lips.
    Round and desperate.

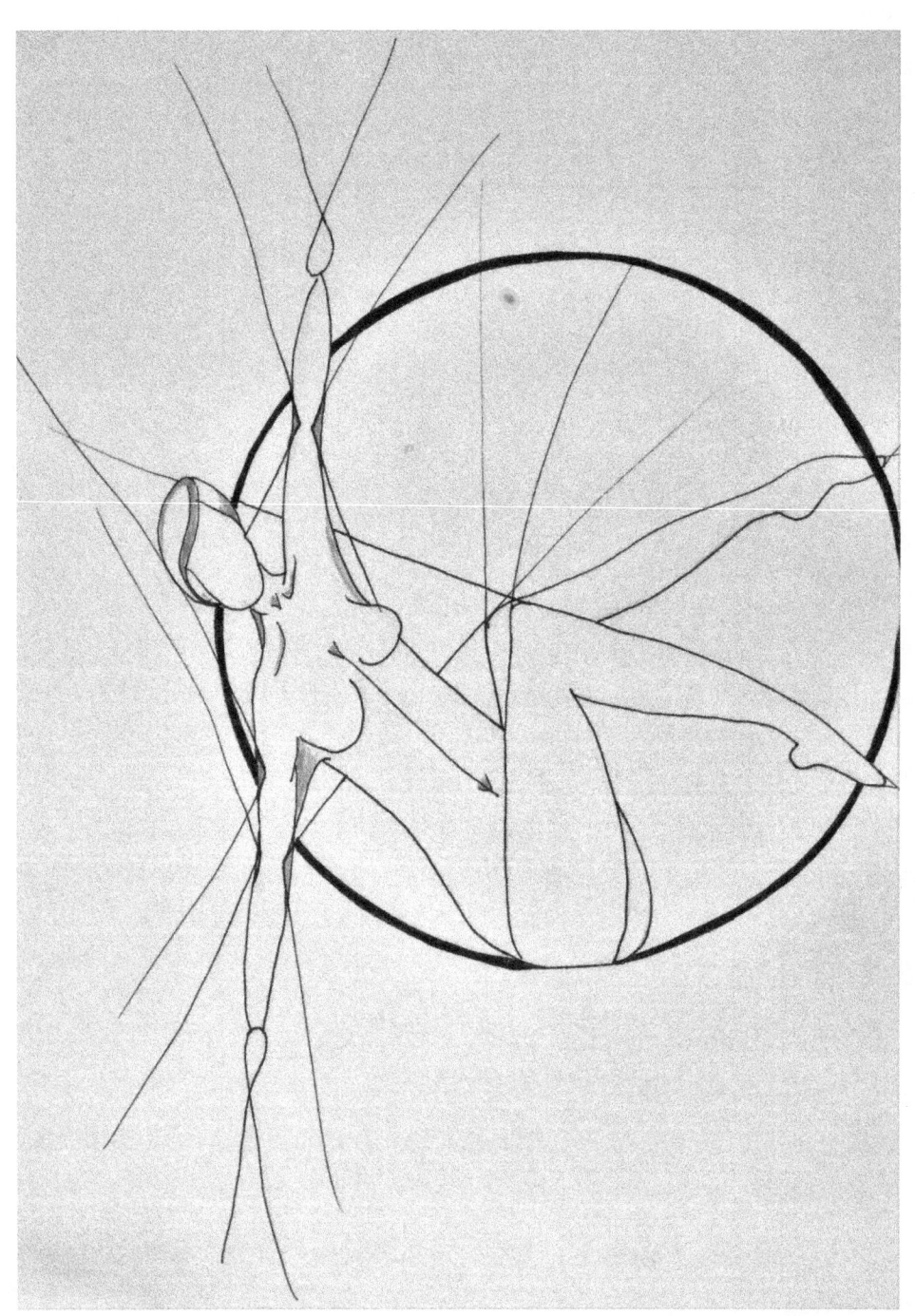

April 26, 2017
Executive Order 13792
Review of Designations Under the Antiquities Act

Untitled

I guess it was a bench
where I pretended you proposed to me,
turning my spirit over and over
in your hands
like kneading soft dough
into a workable start.

We were on the cliffs
over the sea.
Somewhere else there would have been a long pier,
letting a carnival ride her back
like a fantasy city on a turtle.
There would've been music,
a high, tilt-a-whirl tune.

Yes, I still live.
There was nothing left for these ladder bones,
these fleshy expanding hands,
these feet that will not dance.

April 27, 2017
Executive Order 13793
Improving Accountability and Whistleblower Protection at the Department of Veterans Affairs

How Today Finds Me

1
the sound of gnats, swarming
tiny motor flies
or Nanobots to aid your body's farewell
the heat coils to its own smoke signal
confetti, a paper ash flurry
a celebration of doves shot-gunned out of flight

there is glass between you and the street
this moment is uninhabitable
the division is not enough distance
swelter clutches your frame
kissing your face
the heat of an unwelcome lover

this is the shape of a flag
a mouth sucked dry
a set of arms that end in a gun,
hands defined as grip

2
there is bad coffee
it is a constant
in all the meetings, you can be promised
smoke tang and bad coffee
the blonde is neither home nor hearth,
a furnace, heat but no comfort
in this body like scaffolding
this body for climbing out of this
while

the blonde is a place-marker,
a red curve,
a bad cup of coffee, and she deserves more
than to be the blonde in the story
you did not have enough grace left in you to grant her that

when the stranger asks, *how does the day find you*
you say, *the same as all the others*
what you mean is that all the days are stacked up
behind you like cordwood
waiting for one hungry match
the heat of an unwelcome lover

April 28, 2017
Executive Order 13794
Establishment of the American Technology Council

Language

Sometimes I think of your hair still blonde and hanging in sallow curls against your child's cheek. It pulls out all the raw mothering from me wishing to scrub you into soft cleanliness again, scrape away neglect with love like fear. When did you stop squishing grown-up faces with both grubby hands desperate for eye contact? Your blue and sparkling hungry wells. A kiss would be too much, an unfiltered spirit on a parched throat. You have not acquired the pallet to love untested. Cut your curls to the quick and paint them black. Replace your bones with stone, the granite set joints scraping as you breathe. This pile of dust, an exhalation that meant sorry. This one, hello.

April 29, 2017
Executive Order 13795
Implementing an America-First Offshore Energy Strategy

Berth

somewhere
on the coast
there's a berth
a place where the battleship comes in
and where all the fucking
like the war is over
finally starts
it's the concrete space where your feet should be able to plant
but you still have to run
run towards wetsalttearmouth
because your sea-legs haven't stopped pulling you forward
movement the only thing that stops you from falling face first into the earth
each frantic stumble an act of faith
somebody has to catch you
you've forgotten how to stand
the sea has been your cradle for so long these legs are not for walking
they are for swimming
your wrists are not for holding your hands
they are for slitting
and every time you gesture hello
leaving splatters into the sky
and color the clouds
sunsets of your life setting on itself

somewhere
on the coast
there's a berth
it exists only as a re-entrance place

you cannot be the same as you were
too much has happened since then
kiss someone with your hunger
fall into her with your wet body weak from the torrents of the sea
your blood is blood but also sometimes saltwater
this is then before then
this is then and also now

somewhere
on the coast
there's a berth

it's your birth

April 29, 2017
Executive Order 13796
Addressing Trade Agreement Violations and Abuses

Story Keeper

When he died, he left a skeleton scrimshawed into his body's whale road,
narwhal filled and dragon-edged.

The secrets he wrote on his bones left a patina of swallow yellow.

He turned his love for us into a beauty
not even he could see until it was over.

I see you, spread across his femur, as a mermaid in repose.

I am an ocean away, segmented across rib cage.

If we had asked him while he still lived, he would've told us
that it was not his body that separates us.

We would not have believed him.

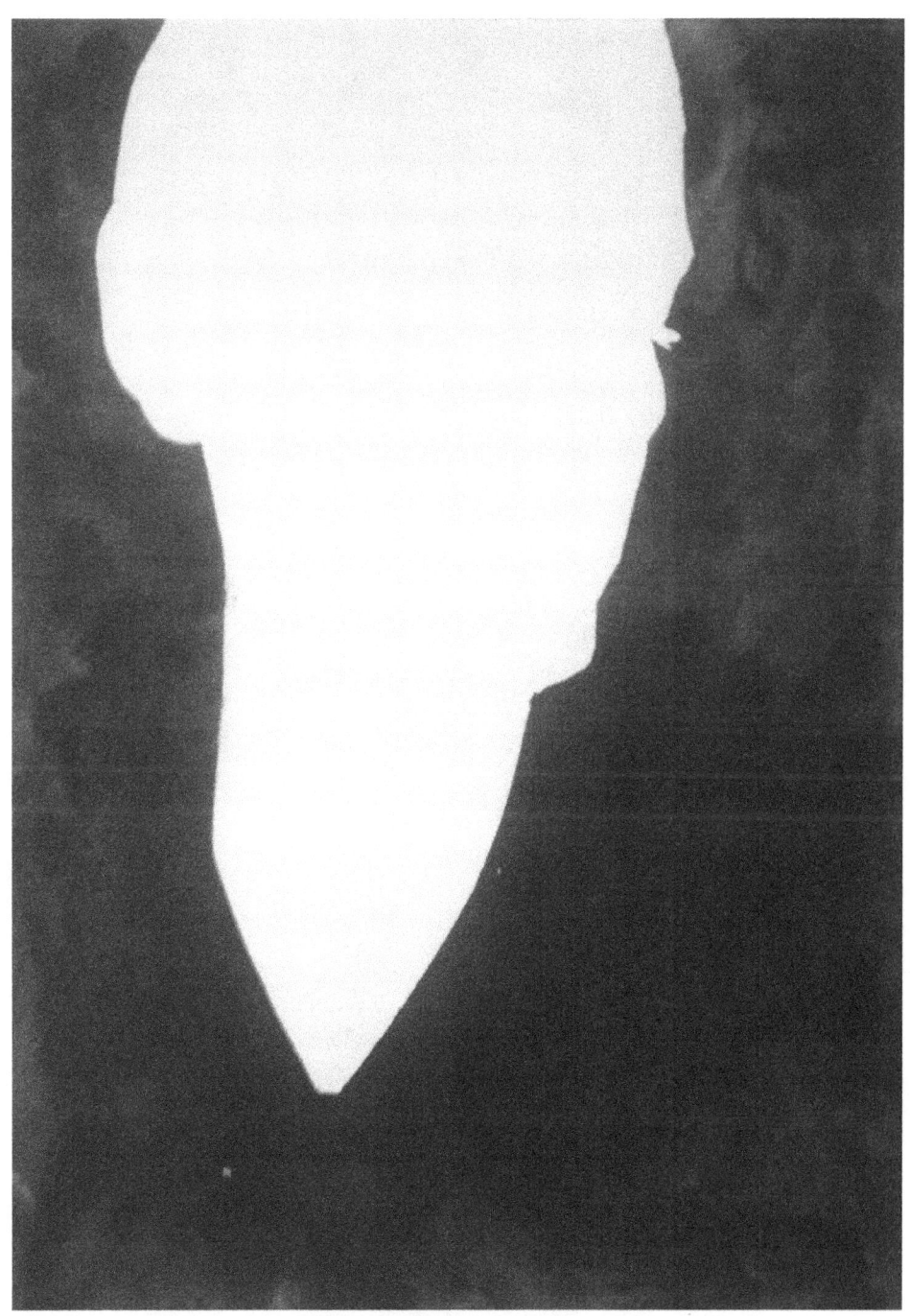

April 29, 2017
Executive Order 13797
Establishment of Office of Trade and Manufacturing Policy

So, You're Living in a Weekly Rental

So, you're living in a weekly rental
with a woman and a child,
neither are yours.
You sleep on the couch
and pay all the rent.

It's the summer,
of overnights at the print factory,
and heavy steel print plates,
your broken arm,
and the man called Tracker
who lost himself and the deposit to the wind.

You see nothing of the months
as they push their days through heat-haze,
through too many cars in the road,
and the baby's colic cry
in aching spirals,
filling the air with constant static scratch.

Define man as one who protects mother and child.
Accept in any mother to replace the ghost of Christmas past.
Use child to scry for future.

That voice in your ears is your own;
taste on your lips, a promise;
the tick of the clock, my heart pacing out the path to your forever;

take the long way.

May 4, 2017
Executive Order 13798
Promoting Free Speech and Religious Liberty

The President Explains Promise-Keeping to a Dreamer

March 1: Danielle Vargas speaks out, tells on the Dream voice she has. Or a dream of a voice.

March 1: Detained for 7 days. Released, but Deportation Order still stands. No hearing scheduled.

No hearing.

May 11, 2017
Executive Order 13799
Establishment of Presidential Advisory Commission on Election Integrity

Render

But still, he says,

    Let's hollow kiss each other's throats closed
    Stuff our mouths
        with tongues
        and seawater
        and sticky childhood
    Till all endings untuck themselves
        from your underskirts
    And why do they call them slips anyway
        if not to slip off
        to hoist up the flagpole
        and let virgin surrender lose
        in the slipstream of…
    Sometimes you can feel the world moving
        but not so much in the slipping of gravel beneath your feet
        as how the wind won't stop seeking out your last breath
    Let your last breath be the cry that raw throats me
        that forever steals the grace from my voice
        and rewrites the loss of you as my own name

May 11, 2017
Executive Order 13800
Strengthening the Cybersecurity of Federal Networks and Critical Infrastructure

This Love

this love's violence of breath
statue standing, icicle cradled on our language

I don't prompt well
verb, noun, adjective

the starless girl in firefly lit panties
trembling with rug burns and bug bites

we are flightless hands
grabbing too hungrily into the earth
turning torn vows into rental properties
have to code the trees in, leaf by leaf, to ensure they still seem real

the coincidence of failures intersect themselves into war games
stumbling into victory, our faces finger-painted nimbostratus camouflage

I have replaced my molars with only the finest dead turncoats
Brutus and Cassius gnash themselves at the back of my kisses
Judas, buried head first, kicks the Morse code for **MERCY** against my tongue

June 15, 2017
Executive Order 13801
Expanding Apprenticeships in America

Norman Rockwell's *The Happy Plumber*

At 4, Bobby told me his daddy was a superhero,
because he wore a red shirt and overalls every day.
We would watch his back walking the sidewalk,
climbing the hill toward his ride to work.

Apprentice good guys didn't warrant a company truck.
Had to provide their own wrenches.

June 21, 2017
Executive Order 13802
Amendment of Executive Order 13597

Being Pregnant at Papa's Funeral

On my grave,
there will be stones—
the craggy-edged weight of holding a body into permanence.
Children,
grandchildren,
of my headstone,
stacked precarious hills of sorrow.
Our deaths are grey and white prayer walls—
a lifetime of memories,
tucked as scraps of words in the cracks of our bones.

This graveyard is flowers.
The violent beauty of crimson nasturtium,
street corner Valencia oranges.
The abundance of garden and feast.
Take with you to the coffin
the taste of pan dulce
and rosewater hands.
Prayer as celebration.

When I was a swollen fig
and your death could color sunrise,
I regretted having already named my son after a different body—
longed to hold on to yours while all the flowers faded.

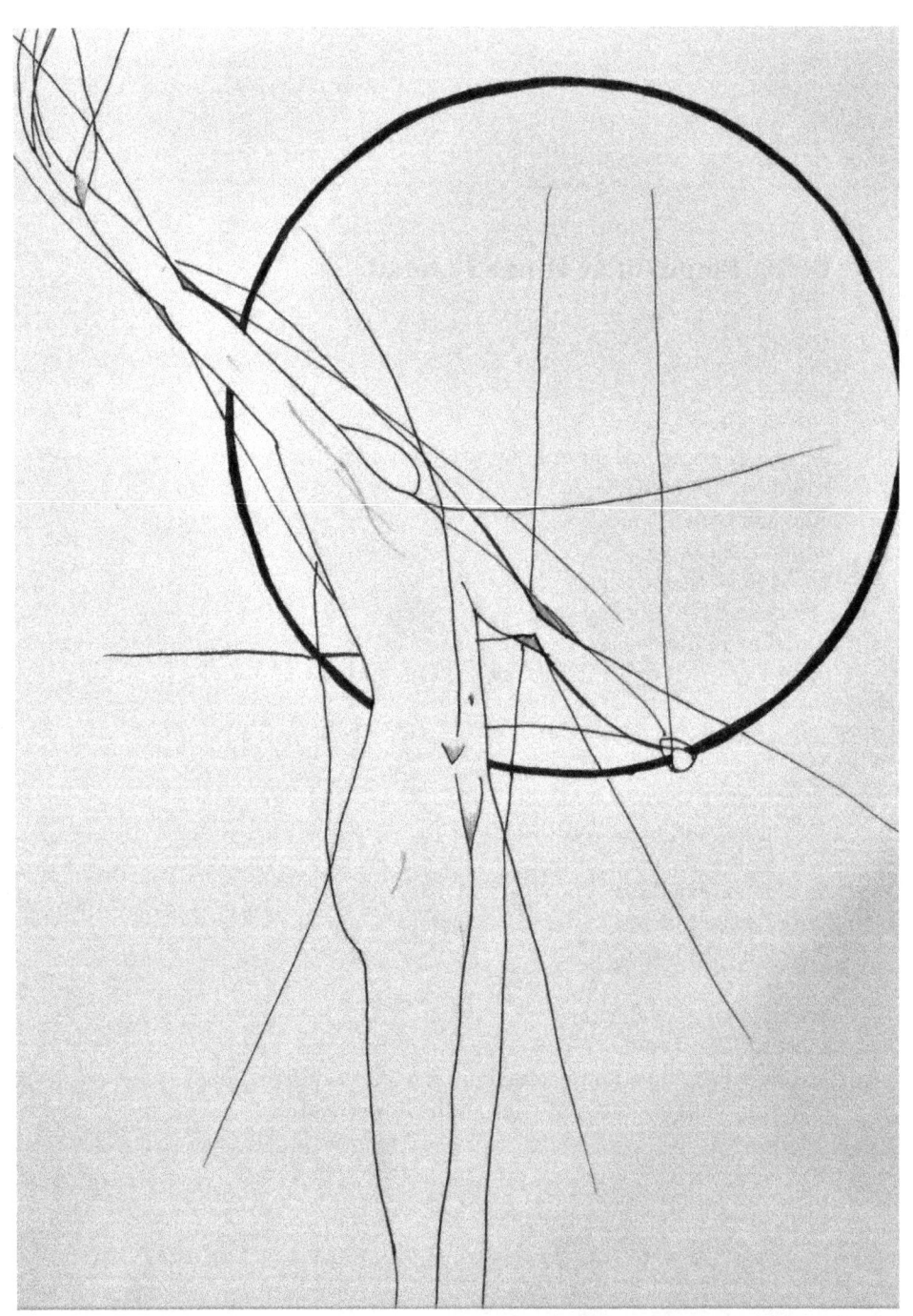

June 30, 2017
Executive Order 13803
Revival of the National Space Council

Stardust

Pretend each lover,
dressed in the powdery embers and luminous expanse
of their own stardust,
comes into view. Rises as constellations,
pantheon of your body's movement through space.
Call your history night sky.
Stars' vibration pulls at heartstring music, drum and lyre.
Percussion and siren song. Accelerando as petition.
Full body embrace of cello as aria of concord.
Forgive yourself your orchestra,
this flood of life and sound,
your body, song.

You were born in the collision of love's gravity.
Bodies compelled to impact and create new object.
You were as nebula pulling itself from matter to substance.
This is the weight of existence, a birthright of physics.
Pretend each lover, worthy of the luminous expense
of their own stardust,
is a gift revealed at egotide for the resting of oneself.
Forgive yourself your melody.
You, like Shubert, to his Symphony will die
unfinished and perfect.
Pretend each love worthy.
Your body,
    stardust,
        song.

July 11, 2017
Executive Order 13804
Amendment of Executive Order 13761

Sepia

She,
and it must always be a she,
is finally held still,
pinned to the page
and glossed over in wood tones.

Can we then
    replace our wings with tresses,
    cascade our flight down our narrow spines,
    filigree ourselves to the earth
        like staying is the same as growing?

Is it a birch
that sprays honeyed leaves?
Her eyes,
dappled forest walls, sunlight
etched permanent.

Embroider my belly into swelling;
my breasts dropping muskmellons.

Will I burst open?
    Splitting and spilling out
        with all my terrible ripeness?

If we were real,
we would be mahogany shadow,
stained as tangles in the knots of
her marble hair. None of us are waves.
We are too rooted in the her for that.

July 19, 2017
Executive Order 13805
Establishing a Presidential Advisory Council on Infrastructure

Long Term House Issues

Baseboard in mudroom, waterlogged.
Missing knob on the stove, left side.
The index finger is still stuck in the u-bend of the main bathroom sink.
I stuffed all my eyelashes into your good work shoes.
They are great for arched eyebrow support.
Your eyes are an Empire State Building full of windows slid off of their tracks.
(Landlord issue?)
Our son's baby teeth click in the winds, scaring raccoons off the porch.
He sucked my chest dry and built his own crib from my cage.
Backdoor sticks on sunny days.
Fans, forgetting how to spin upwards, are permanently stuck on winter,
    pushing your hot lips down from the ceiling.
Both shower heads sing: *Oh, I love to go swimmin' with bowlegged wimmen.*
My body, a bridge, carries these weights.
Your hands keep crawling onto my side of the bed
and stitching me back together
    with the straight ribbon from our eldest child's head.

July 21, 2017
Executive Order 13806
Assessing and Strengthening the Manufacturing and Defense Industrial Base and Supply Chain Resiliency of the United States

Seven Lies
for an insomniac on cheap whiskey nights

The stars are stand-ins,
fillers for gods,
just so we can figure out how to properly light the love scenes.

The night grows everything bigger,
carrying you with it,
to fill up all the newfound space.

The music is for you.
So are the crickets, the moon, and her smile.

If you fall asleep now,
tomorrow might still be worth something.

She remembers you;
he does not.

We can hold ourselves here,
paint our mouths into silence.
We can be skylines, doll faces, ceramic shepherds, still fruit, lace curtains.

She is coming back. I promise.

August 15, 2017
Executive Order 13807
Establishing Discipline and Accountability in the Environmental Review and Permitting Process
for Infrastructure

Prompt

Make a list of five detailed social interactions.

- Casual tea at your kitchen table
- Being stuck at the worst table of a wedding reception
- A PTA meeting in the middle school gym
- Passover Seder with the same Haggadah you grew up with
- A seventh date

Make a list of five public, impersonal events that have left you gut-tied and choking on your own inactive hands.
Pick one from each list. Interact with the events in a social structure you chose.

Invite a public shooting to Passover (not the shooter; the event itself).
Tell the bullets about the afikomen.
Ask them if they search for flesh
the same way you did the napkin wrapped wafer.
Ask them if they knew of any better ways to find the ending of the story.

Take Flint's leaded water on a seventh date.
Explain to yourself why you are still here,
kissing water that tastes like your teeth falling out
and filling your mouth with blood.
Look at the other diners.
Do they know you are not safe?
Do they worry for you?
Why won't they do anything?

August 25, 2017
Executive Order 13808
Imposing Sanctions with Respect to the Situation in Venezuela

Parts

Day 1 was the heat haze of a Thursday afternoon.
They tumbled down without the protection of a decent cloud cover,
hit pavement, cars, upturned faces.
No blood or ragged edges.
Just the warm sounding soft splat of unused ears collapsing to the ground.

Despite the health warnings, we snuck the flaccid curves
to our secret keeping places,
bedroom closets, the gazebo in Maria's backyard.
Studied the chrysanthemum curls,
crevices, looked for the magic numbers or Italian style patterns
in the flatten shells.
The backs were slick, smooth skin, Ken's crotch clean,
but the lobes, peach-down fullness on the tongues, all tasted of former owners.
We recognized that without knowledge,
like finding Christmas in the forest.

Friday it was eyelashes. They were a deluge, still wet with...
They got tangled in everything, burrowed into fabric, stowed away
in our agreements and hungry-mouthed make-up sex.

Within a week, pedestrians in Arizona used Abuelita's hands as ID cards,
always palm side up. In South Korea and Garden Grove they replaced
the corners of mouths with the upturned tics of fallen laughter,
borrowing a picture of a smile to avoid the *Hey baby, why so sad?*
Let's have a grin.
Give us happy. Give us. Least you can do is fake it.

I hunted up PCH, scavenging in the wetlands for your collarbone.

Suburban teens hid in bathrooms back with scooped up femurs—
gave themselves bone marrow transplant to increase density.

Day 17, we stretched new shoes with old feet.
Day 28, everyone had blue eyes and horn-rimmed glasses.
By the 32nd Day we forgot which days belonged to Thor or the Sun—
there were HipsDay, ElbowsDay, the day we rolled found teeth
for initiative.
On the 40th day, fingerprints shook down,
little white whirl snowflakes covered everything.
There were no more culpable parties.
All the ID scans came back empty.

I found your bottom lip in a coffee shop.
The narrow girl that wore it worried it constantly,
chewing the salted caramel strip in your sleep.
Says that and a cup of coffee might give her the energy to head home.
Spare some change?

August 28, 2017
Letter to Congress and Executive Order 13809
Restoring State, Tribal, and Local Law Enforcement's Access to Life-Saving Equipment and Resources

How Not to Silence a Mother
after Wayman Barnes' How to Not Break-up with Margaret

1. Never shush her during rainstorms. She will turn the worries inward, grind lightning bolts between her molars, cradling scorch marks on her tongue. You will feel quilts when she jumps at the sudden gush of water from the faucet. Your hands will shake while you scrub the dishes in the quiet until you drop the 'very forespecial' plate. The one with the spidery blue ivy vines running across the white.

2. Try not to look her in the eye. You will see her paint you the shadow grey/sunset orange of two ex-husbands and one dead father.

3. Remind yourself of the value of quiet. That her words are an intrusion, an engagement you have not agreed to.

4. Do not fix yourself a drink. *See number 2.*

5. No, not even a beer.

6. Ignore the holes in her favorite dress. The red flowered one that reminds her of living in Malibu with her best friend and a deep-sea diver that looked nothing like your father.

7. Pretend you aren't wearing wisps of her grey, pinned at your own hairline by time and your own children.

8. Avoid looking at the pictures on the wall. You will realize there are none with you and your brother in the same frame. You are portraits on opposite sides of the room, smiling each other down. It's not her fault anyway and it will just piss you off.

9. Stop listening to her hands whispering condolences to each other. They have been hosting a memorial for your laughter for years and wouldn't know how to stop now.

10. Ignore the tears running down your cheeks.

11. Keep from calling her name.

12. Do not apologize.

13. Do not ask her how to spell apologize.

14. Stop feeling like you hit her.

September 20, 2017
Letter to Congress and Executive Order 13810
Imposing Additional Sanctions with Respect to North Korea

Sailor

Inside, the coil is slick and iridescent.
Can a living fossil fall in love
after seeing her nautilus face
reflected 1000 times over
on the walls of her armor?
There is safety in numbers.

We are not the blue-grey sky.
We are not the rainbows' marble against her skin.

The nautilus is the only
creature that can be ripped
from the ocean floor
and thrust to the sky without
dying.

We are not the water's pressured kiss.
We are the lie of air.

September 29, 2017
Letter to Congress and Executive Order 13811
Continuance of Certain Federal Advisory Committees

Pre-Script

Before the first date lobster rolls
and the food truck, its royal
blue and purple, salt scrubbed
to seaside carnival fade.

Before the Jeep
driver's side lock always-stuck,
metal tongue unwilling
to give up the back-of-the-teeth tang
of a dark place it could fill.

Before the tangle of want and
loneliness made you unable to
recognize red lights or
EXIT signs.

You cradled scoops of pier water
in hands gobbleted in the cold,
understood mermaids singing sailors
to their arms, holding in the wild
embrace of never being alone.

September 29, 2017
Executive Order 13812
Revocation of Executive Order Creating Labor-Management Forum

Blue

1
Can sorrow be a vibrant viscosity?
Or a rising fume that pulls air from lungs to turpentine them onto garage walls?
Is it work-shirts and window trim?
The sky's goodbye to the day?

Is it water? This paint between our hands and teeth.
Is it teeth?

2
When I was a child, my stepfather was a house painter,
until he was a fall-off-of-a-ladder and a workman's-comp case.
He specialized in the fine, fiddly trim—straight lined ornamentation of a home.
At night, he sat at a high drafting table we could not afford and sketched for hours.
Dancing other people's cartoon figures through the pot smoke.

3
I cannot straight line the blue of you.
It rivers into curves in my fingers.
You are deluge and outpouring.
You are water and think cerulean paint.
I am teeth and hands. Grip and mine, mine, mine.

4
Is your art of value?
Are you?
Is it water?
Does this paint we cannot afford keep a body alive?
Who owns these blue spattered fingers?

Oct 12, 2017
Executive Order 13813
Promoting Healthcare Choice and Competition Across the United States

Diagnosis: Unspecified Effects of Drowning and Nonfatal Submersion, Initial Encounter

The stove top clicks out its staccato beginning.
My hand pauses at the knob,
mind untethers,
kites above me,
     long
       languid
          loops
  in the kitchen fan's
     updraft.
Until the pilot light catches the air
in a sudden heated fireflower
that starts me back.

This is how we heat the water,
how we make the bath,
to submerge the eggs,
and wait,
and wait.
Till white oval float to the surface.
Bob in the rolling bubbles.
And wait.
Till they can be pulled from the shell,
and the soft flesh,
still wet from death,
pushes back against my fingertips,
and I am on the tile floor clasping
these broken bodies to my chest,
crying for lost children floating in hot baths.
Their soft flesh still wet.

October 20, 2017
Executive Order 13814
Amending Executive Order 13223

Sea Voyage

1. Stop writing poems about her

2. Unteach your fingertips the feel of her new fallen in your bed. Untangle the Y of her name from the raven feathers of your hair. Let your chest breathe again, rise and fall without the weight of her coiled up against you like the snowy albatross. She was only bad luck when you shot her out of the sky, tried to hold onto her, thought of her a sustenance instead of sea foam.

3. Let sorrow be your lover; she is more faithful.

October 24, 2017
Executive Order 13815
Resuming the United States Refugee Admissions Program with Enhanced Vetting Capabilities

Placeholder

You have to understand, no one puts their children in a boat unless the water is safer than the land.

No one leaves home unless home is the mouth of a shark.

   — Warsan Shire, *Home*

The thing about my tits is
     every child that made it to them is still alive.
     I can almost say the same for every lover.

Never read stories about Mengele while pregnant—
     the babies will still root,
     gasping and crying at taped down Jewish breasts,

     until they won't.

These are make-up tits,
     or apology breasts—
     they can never comfort enough weary heads to balance this
weight, the loss of a generation that cried out
     until they didn't.

If you define me by fertility I am fecund until fetid.
     We are swollen bellies and swallowed tongues.

What I have learned in the last several days:

Someday, child, people will try to reclaim the knife that is stuck in your side.

Howl-mouth at you: it was a tool before it was a weapon.
Your family's blood will spill to the earth from re-opened wounds.
They will be upset you cried the loss of a tool,
       claim they have the right to use it.
They will be angry that you leave your red handprints all over the walls,
on their clothes,
on their fine,
fine
trim.

This body takes up space because it must.

I am holding a place open until it can be filled again.

December 8, 2017
Executive Order 13816
Revising the Seal for the National Credit Union Administration

Letter to B~

Poets only ever seem to write about
the hungry tangle of a kiss
                              the sea at night,
                                                and loss.

They only ever write about you.

December 20, 2017
Executive Order 13817
A Federal Strategy to Ensure Secure and Reliable Supplies of Critical Minerals

Snake Eaters

I placed his tongue on my own,
so he could lap up the water words that flowed.
The choking,
as his lithe body struggled to navigate the rapids of my throat,
was inevitable.
He tells me now I was crying,
and the sorrow carved the path out too wide,
letting each word echo in the ruins of my ribcage.
Or it was the wind.

He never knows the difference.

December 21, 2017
Executive Order 13818
Blocking the Property of Persons Involved in Serious Human Rights Abuse or Corruption

Michael Powell's *Peeping Tom*

The camera doesn't rape or even possess, though it may presume, intrude, trespass, distort, exploit and, at the farthest reaches of metaphor, assassinate—all activities that, unlike the sexual push and shove, can be conducted from a distance, and with some detachment.

    — Susan Sontag, On Photography

My eyes are not shattering glass windows
or mirrors splintered into red lights,
meaning both stop and for sale at once.
They are screwed up fist punching themselves black.
We say survivor like a carnival booth consolation prize.
It was never soft and hunger-filling as advertised.
I am a vivid slash across the fading of history,
refusing to stay pinned in the photograph,
still screaming, *fuck*, over and over.
The thing they don't tell you is some nights are black holes
bookended by an all-teeth shark smile
and the turquoise trim of a hotel
you have never seen before.
That in the only evidence of that night
is a picture of you,
still in the bar,
smiling.

The thing about grief nobody tells you is
you resent every step.

December 22, 2017
Executive Order 13819
Adjustments of Certain Rates of Pay

Skeleton Key

She grips the meaty, saucy ribs
between just the tips of her fingers curled to the O's of her hands
and pulls the bites off with the cruel efficiency of sharp-edged teeth
like razors guarding her tongue.

I am this—the long bones that cage
heart and lungs, waiting to be
stripped to chalking white, peel tendon
and ligament, sweet meat sucked
from the core till laid bare like
first rib pulled from first man to make
first woman.

She is quick, scraping teeth to bone,
needle on vinyl crosswise, ship groaning
against moorings, the sweet backhanded
slap of the wrong compliment from
someone you love. She cleaves dinner
from body until there is only bone
left. Aching, curved fingers laid out
on her plate.

If this is all there is, I think, let me die in her mouth.

Acknowledgements

Firstly, thank you to my husband and children for your boundless patience. Or, more accurately, thank you to my husband for patiently running interference with our boundless children.

To my family of blood and family of heart. You make me see a better version of myself ever on the horizon. I promise to never stop reaching for her.

Thank you to Ben Trigg and Steve Ramirez. You may be Two Idiots Peddling Poetry but you do it so well. I am grateful for your love and that your reading has filled me with the words of brilliant poets week-after-week, year-after-year.

Thank you to Phil for letting poets flood the Ugly Mug.

A special thanks to Seth Halbeisen for making me look good, even at the last minute.

And of course, thank you Eric Morago for believing this book belonged out in the world.

* * *

I would like to give a special thanks to my patrons at Patreon. I am so proud of the community we are building and amazed how much each one of you add to that community.

Alexandra Umlas	LeAnne Hunt
Becca Hiraheta	Matthew Rouse
Ben Trigg	Michael Cantin
Betsy Mars	Nancy Lynée Woo
Bryan Banuelos	Nico Paoli
Chelsea Rose	Robin Axworthy
G. Murray Thomas	Sarah ChristianScher
Heather Love	Seth Halbeisen
Heidi Denkers	Sheila Sadr
JL Martindale	Worley Gig Games
Ln Webre	Zaidan Izzuddin Akbar

About the Author

HanaLena Fennel was born in Oregon and raised in California. She has spent most of her life surrounded by people, but slightly misplaced. Brazenly bisexual and aggressively awkward, HanaLena is a mother of three darling dybbuks, three cats, a hedgehog, a betta fish named Caboose, 2 ghost shrimp, one snail, and a dog simultaneously named after a Roman god and an element. After having artwork and poems published in various anthologies and collections (including Moon Tide's own *Dark Ink* horror anthology), she is excited about publishing her first full book of poetry. HanaLena is currently an associate editor for the online literary journal, *FreezeRay*. Her weekly prompts, artwork, and support can found on her Patreon: https://www.patreon.com/HanaLenaFennel

Patrons

Moon Tide Press would like to thank the following people for their support in helping publish the finest poetry from the Southern California region. To sign up as a patron, visit www.moontidepress.com or send an email to publisher@moontidepress.com.

Anonymous
Robin Axworthy
Conner Brenner
Bill Cushing
Susan Davis
Peggy Dobreer
Dennis Gowans
Half Off Books & Brad T. Cox
Jim & Vicky Hoggatt
Ron Koertge & Bianca Richards
Ray & Christi Lacoste
Zachary & Tammy Locklin
Lincoln McElwee
David McIntire
José Enrique Medina
Andrew November
Michael Miller & Rachanee Srisavasdi
Terri Niccum
Ronny & Richard Morago
Jennifer Smith
Andrew Turner
Mariano Zaro

Also Available from Moon Tide Press

Darwin's Garden, Lee Rossi (2019)
Dark Ink: A Poetry Anthology Inspired by Horror (2018)
Drop and Dazzle, Peggy Dobreer (2018)
Junkie Wife, Alexis Rhone Fancher (2018)
The Moon, My Lover, My Mother, & the Dog, Daniel McGinn (2018)
Lullaby of Teeth: An Anthology of Southern California Poetry (2017)
Angels in Seven, Michael Miller (2016)
A Likely Story, Robbi Nester (2014)
Embers on the Stairs, Ruth Bavetta (2014)
The Green of Sunset, John Brantingham (2013)
The Savagery of Bone, Timothy Matthew Perez (2013)
The Silence of Doorways, Sharon Venezio (2013)
Cosmos: An Anthology of Southern California Poetry (2012)
Straws and Shadows, Irena Praitis (2012)
In the Lake of Your Bones, Peggy Dobreer (2012)
I Was Building Up to Something, Susan Davis (2011)
Hopeless Cases, Michael Kramer (2011)
One World, Gail Newman (2011)
What We Ache For, Eric Morago (2010)
Now and Then, Lee Mallory (2009)
Pop Art: An Anthology of Southern California Poetry (2009)
In the Heaven of Never Before, Carine Topal (2008)
A Wild Region, Kate Buckley (2008)
Carving in Bone: An Anthology of Orange County Poetry (2007)
Kindness from a Dark God, Ben Trigg (2007)
A Thin Strand of Lights, Ricki Mandeville (2006)
Sleepyhead Assassins, Mindy Nettifee (2006)
Tide Pools: An Anthology of Orange County Poetry (2006)
Lost American Nights: Lyrics & Poems, Michael Ubaldini (2006)

This page intentionally left blank

This page intentionally left blank

This page intentionally left blank

www.ingramcontent.com/pod-product-compliance
Lightning Source LLC
Chambersburg PA
CBHW031202090426
42736CB00009B/765